AWESOME DOGS

Great Danes

by Chris Bowman

BLASTOFF!
2
READERS

BELLWETHER MEDIA • MINNEAPOLIS, MN

Note to Librarians, Teachers, and Parents:

Blastoff! Readers are carefully developed by literacy experts and combine standards-based content with developmentally appropriate text.

Level 1 provides the most support through repetition of high-frequency words, light text, predictable sentence patterns, and strong visual support.

Level 2 offers early readers a bit more challenge through varied simple sentences, increased text load, and less repetition of high-frequency words.

Level 3 advances early-fluent readers toward fluency through increased text and concept load, less reliance on visuals, longer sentences, and more literary language.

Level 4 builds reading stamina by providing more text per page, increased use of punctuation, greater variation in sentence patterns, and increasingly challenging vocabulary.

Level 5 encourages children to move from "learning to read" to "reading to learn" by providing even more text, varied writing styles, and less familiar topics.

Whichever book is right for your reader, Blastoff! Readers are the perfect books to build confidence and encourage a love of reading that will last a lifetime!

This edition first published in 2016 by Bellwether Media, Inc.

No part of this publication may be reproduced in whole or in part without written permission of the publisher. For information regarding permission, write to Bellwether Media, Inc., Attention: Permissions Department, 5357 Penn Avenue South, Minneapolis, MN 55419.

Library of Congress Cataloging-in-Publication Data

Bowman, Chris, 1990- author.
 Great Danes / by Chris Bowman.
    pages cm. – (Blastoff! Readers. Awesome Dogs)
 Summary: "Relevant images match informative text in this introduction to Great Danes. Intended for students in kindergarten through third grade"–Provided by publisher.
 Audience: Ages 5-8.
 Audience: K to grade 3.
 Includes bibliographical references and index.
 ISBN 978-1-62617-306-4 (hardcover : alk. paper)
 1. Great Dane–Juvenile literature. 2. Dog breeds–Juvenile literature. I. Title. II. Series: Blastoff! Readers. 2, Awesome Dogs.
 SF429.G7B69 2016
 636.73–dc23   2015031575

Table of Contents

What Are Great Danes?	4
History of Great Danes	12
Gentle Giants	18
Glossary	22
To Learn More	23
Index	24

What Are Great Danes?

Great Danes are one of the world's tallest dog **breeds**. They are friendly animals.

Sometimes their name is shortened to Danes.

Danes are very large in size. They have long necks and legs.

6

Their ears flop down over big, rectangular heads. Some ears stick up.

These dogs have short, thick **coats**. Their fur comes in many colors.

Great Dane Coats

blue   black   fawn

Danes can be blue, black, or **fawn**.

mantle

harlequin

Many Great Danes have patterned coats.

Some are **mantle** or **harlequin**. Others are **merle** or **brindle**.

merle

History of Great Danes

Great Danes have an old history. **Ancient** Egyptians drew pictures of big dogs like Danes.

The ancient Chinese wrote about them.

The true Great Dane breed began in Germany during the 1600s.

Germany

N
W · E
S

The dogs hunted wild boars
and guarded people's homes.

During the 1800s, people **bred** the dogs to be more calm. Today, Danes are popular family pets.

Great Dane Profile

big head

large body

long legs

Life Span: 7 to 10 years

Trainability:

1 2 3 4 5 6

Hardest to train   Easiest to train

The **American Kennel Club** places them in the **Working Group**.

Gentle Giants

Great Danes love to be with people. Some work as **therapy dogs**.

Their large size and calm nature
are comforting to people.

These dogs are sometimes called gentle giants. Danes are gentle with children and other pets.

Many Danes try to be lap dogs even though they are huge!

Glossary

American Kennel Club—an organization that keeps track of dog breeds in the United States

ancient—from long ago

bred—purposely mated two dogs to make puppies with certain qualities

breeds—types of dogs

brindle—a solid coat color mixed with streaks or spots of another color

coats—the hair or fur covering some animals

fawn—a light brown color

harlequin—a pattern that is mostly white with black spots

mantle—a pattern that is mostly black with a white snout, neck, chest, and feet

merle—a pattern that is one solid color with patches and spots of another color

therapy dogs—dogs that comfort people who are sick, hurt, or have a disability

Working Group—a group of dog breeds that have a history of performing jobs for people

To Learn More

AT THE LIBRARY
Johnson, Jinny. *Great Dane*. Mankato, Minn.: Smart
Apple Media, 2015.

Landau, Elaine. *Great Danes Are the Best!*
Minneapolis, Minn.: Lerner Publications, Co., 2011.

Rajczak, Kristen. *Great Danes*. New York, N.Y.:
Gareth Stevens Pub., 2012.

ON THE WEB
Learning more about Great Danes
is as easy as 1, 2, 3.

1. Go to www.factsurfer.com.

2. Enter "Great Danes" into the search box.

3. Click the "Surf" button and you will see a
   list of related web sites.

With factsurfer.com, finding more
information is just a click away.

Index

American Kennel
   Club, 17
bred, 16
breeds, 4, 14
children, 20
Chinese, 13
coats, 8, 9, 10
colors, 8, 9
ears, 7
Egyptians, 12
fur, 8
Germany, 14
guarded, 15
heads, 7, 17
hunted, 15
lap dogs, 21
legs, 6, 17
life span, 17
nature, 19

necks, 6
nicknames, 5, 20
patterns, 10, 11
pets, 16, 20
size, 4, 6, 12, 17, 19,
   21
therapy dogs, 18
trainability, 17
wild boars, 15
work, 18
Working Group, 17